He Believed

(Those Words His Mother Said)

Annette Turner

Illustrated by: Madison Mizelle

AuthorHouse™
1663 Liberty Drive
Bloomington, IN 47403
www.authorhouse.com
Phone: 1 (800) 839-8640

Because of the dynamic nature of the Internet, any web addresses or links contained in this book may have changed
since publication and may no longer be valid. The views expressed in this work are solely those of the author and do
not necessarily reflect the views of the publisher, and the publisher hereby disclaims any responsibility for them.

Any people depicted in stock imagery provided by Getty Images are models,
and such images are being used for illustrative purposes only.
Certain stock imagery © Getty Images.

This book is printed on acid-free paper.

ISBN: 978-1-7283-3412-7 (sc)
ISBN: 978-1-7283-3413-4 (e)

Print information available on the last page.

Published by AuthorHouse 10/29/2019

authorHOUSE®

He Believed
(Those Words His Mother Said)

Sammy was a silly goose,
As sweet as he could be.
He liked to play and run around
To see what he could see.

Through the grass he'd run and play
From daylight until dusk.
Not worrying 'bout anything.
Not giving thought to much.

He went along his merry way
One bright and sunny day.
He came upon a pretty pond,
As he ran and played.

He'd seen this pond a hundred times,
As he'd run around.
He thought he heard it rumble
Though it didn't make a sound.

A little while he looked at it,
It's beauty and it's calm,
Until his best friend Sara came,
And their friend Woodchuck Tom.

Sara was his favorite friend,
A pretty little pup.
She smiled and yelped and danced a bit,
And sweetly said, "What's up?"

"I'm just hanging out today,"
Said Sammy with a shrug.
He waddled closer to the pond
And gave his friend a hug.

They went along their merry way
To see what they could see.
Not giving thought to anything,
As pure as they were free.

No one thought about the day
They might get into trouble.
No one ever thought about
A fear, a pain, or struggle.

They played a little silly game
That Woodchuck Tom made up.
They ran and chased around the pond
To see who'd catch more bugs.

As they played the silly game,
They didn't even know.
The pond was very dangerous,
And they were very close.

Sara jumped to catch a bug,
Right at the water's edge.
She slipped and rolled and tumbled,
And fell right through the hedge.

She went into the water
With a big and noisy splash.
Woodchuck Tom and Sammy
Ran right to her in a flash.

All they saw was water,
So they didn't know what to do.
Sammy'd never swam before.
Woodchuck Tom turned blue.

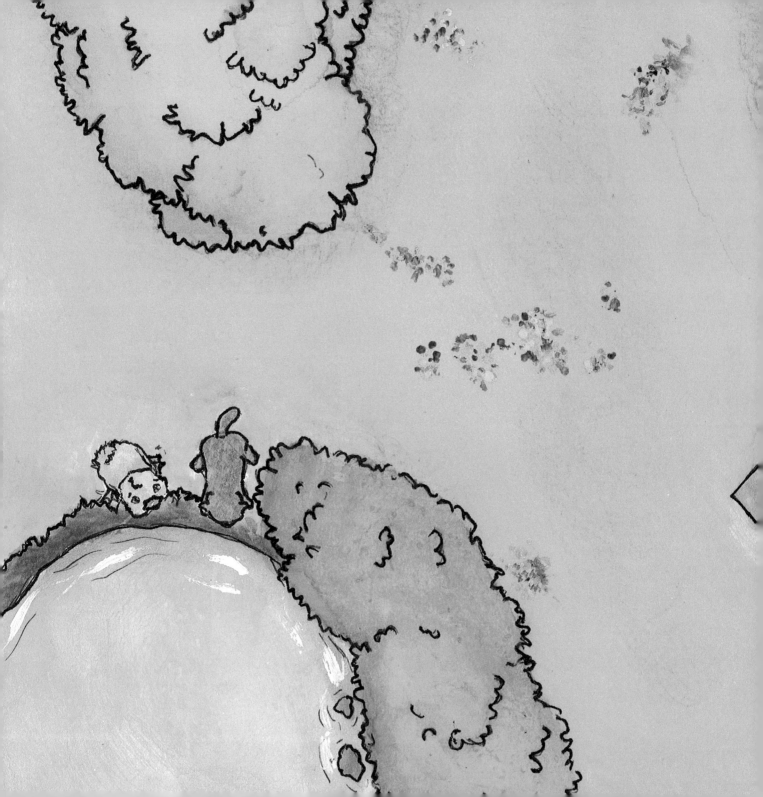

Sammy started crying
As he tried to make a plan.
He wished he had his mother there
To hold onto his hand.

He looked up and imagined
His precious mother's face.
He felt like such a tiny thing
In this enormous place.

Right then a thought came to him,
Those words his mother said,
"If you ever have a problem,
Turn to God and bow your head."

"Don't be scared to jump right in.
Don't quit when you're in fear.
Believe and pray and trust in him
He'll always be right here."

He thought of all the times he'd heard
His mother's words of faith.
He'd never really thought about
A fear he'd have to face.

But all at once he'd came upon
A fear he'd always had.
He hadn't even known it,
But the water scared him bad.

Because he'd never given thought
To things along his way,
He didn't know which words to use,
But bowed his head to pray.

"God I turn and pray to You.
I'm in a time of need.
I need Your help to see me through.
Please kindly take the lead."

Right then he felt some comfort,
And he felt a sense of peace.
He knew that he could do it.
He would focus and believe.

He turned around and smiled,
And he said to Woodchuck Tom,
"I'm going in the water now,
Please pray we all stay calm."

He took a breath and jumped right in,
And boldly faced his fear.
He'd heard those words his mother said
And *knew* that God was here.

He splashed and dunked and gasped,
Felt like he was in some trouble.
He couldn't see a single thing,
Except for all the bubbles.

Sara treaded water,
Though she couldn't seem to swim.
"Be careful Sam! I'm over here!"
She yelled out to her friend.

Sammy couldn't hear
With all the splashing going on.
He prayed he was not drowning
In the water all alone.

"Please help me Lord! I **know** you're here!
My precious mother told me.
She leans on You in times of need.
She more than once has shown me."

The water seemed to calm a bit.
The bubbles went away.
He felt the presence of the Lord.
And knew he was okay.

Right then he started floating
On the surface of the pond.
He could see his best friend Sara now,
And their friend Woodchuck Tom.

He floated over to her,
And he helped her to the bank.
He felt relief and happiness,
And gave to God his thanks.

He knew that what had happened
Was the mighty grace of God.
He told his friends beside him
And he then began to sob.

He'd always been a carefree soul,
Not looking far ahead.
He couldn't help but think about
Those words his mother said.

He thought of all the times he'd seen
His mother kneel to pray.
He'd never really thought about it
Much until today.

He took his best friend Sara's paw,
And Woodchuck Tom by his.
They bowed their heads together,
And from Sammy they heard this.

"Dear Lord I love you dearly
On this blessed happy day.
I thank You for Your mercy
As You surely led the way."

"You are my inspiration.
You're the way to hope and truth.
My mother said You are the One,
She led me straight to You."

"I ask You to forgive me please
For all my wayward sins.
I give my heart and soul to You.
Please kindly take me in."

They raised their heads and smiled,
And they gave each other hugs.
They were glad they'd run and played
The little silly game with bugs.

Today was the beginning.
A time to look ahead.
The day he'd stopped and thought about
Those words his mother said.

About the Author

Annette Turner was born on January 3, 1967 in Stuart, Virginia. She is married to her husband of 23 years, and has 3 children and 4 grandchildren. Annette graduated from Virginia Tech in 1990 with a bachelor's degree in Health and Physical Education, and in 1997 with a master's degree in Special Education. She is currently in her 23rd year of teaching in Stokes County, North Carolina. Annette enjoys spending time with her family and writing children's books.

About the Illustrator

Madison Mizelle is a 14 year old student at Piney Grove Middle School in Stokes County, North Carolina. She is the youngest of 8 children in her family, and enjoys drawing and painting of all types. She is a gifted illustrator at a very young age, and aspires to continue illustrating children's books.

Printed in the United States
By Bookmasters